ETERNAL SALVATION

"Verily, verily, I say unto you, He that heareth my word, and believeth on him that sent me, hath everlasting life, and shall not come into condemnation; but is passed from death unto life." John 5:24

LEO R. LAVINKA

Copyright © 2020 by Leo R. LaVinka
All Rights Reserved
Printed in the United States of America
January, 2020

REL067030: Religion: Christian Theology – Apologetics.

ISBN 978-1-7341927-9-7

All Scripture quotes are from the King James Bible.

No part of this work may be reproduced without the expressed consent of the publisher, except for brief quotes, whether by electronic, photocopying, recording, or information storage and retrieval systems.

Address All Inquiries To:
THE OLD PATHS PUBLICATIONS, Inc.
142 Gold Flume Way
Cleveland, Georgia, U.S.A. 30528

Web: www.theoldpathspublications.com
E-mail: TOP@theoldpathspublications.com

1.0

DEDICATION

H. D. & Patricia Williams

I dedicate this book to Dr. H.D. Williams and his wife, Patricia. Currently they are directors of "The Old Paths Publications," which specializes in print-on-demand (POD) and ebooks. Dr. Williams also teaches the Adult Sunday School Class at Zion Hill Baptist Church in Cleveland, Georgia. He is the author of numerous books, mostly defending the King James Bible (KJV). He recently received a very high honor by being awarded for the year 2019 Defender of Scripture from the King James Bible Research Council. This award was merited for his strong defense of the Textus Receptus and the King James Bible. They were instrumental in encouraging me to write three books, "Are You Ready?," "Answered Prayers," and this book. They spend hours on formatting, developing the cover, editing, preparing, and publishing only good, solid Christian books. They are always eager to perform any duty which will further the gospel of Jesus Christ. Knowing them is a great honor. My wife and I are fortunate to be able to call them our friends.

ETERNAL SALVATION

FOREWORD

In our nation where the gospel of God can be read and heard, there are still many lost people, and many others who claim to be Christians, yet they do not believe you can have eternal salvation. Still others believe you can lose your salvation once you have it. To believe the Bible and its truth is even now being taught by some that it contains errors and cannot be totally relied upon. There are so many perverted translations that some claim you can't be sure which is the original preserved copy. Some readily accept perverted texts as the basis for their beliefs and declare them to be the best. When these things occur, God's truth becomes obscured and in many verses are deleted and/or added to. It is no wonder that believing in eternal salvation is becoming lost and people doubt their salvation. They are doomed to go through their life with no assurance. May God help all of us to remember a few years back when most people believed the Bible and accepted it as God's truth without harboring any doubt. May those continue in the faith and declare it so that all can hear. God has preserved his Word, the Holy King James version of the Bible for English speaking people. Believe it. You <u>can</u> know you have "Eternal Security."

ETERNAL SALVATION

TABLE OF CONTENTS

DEDICATION	3
FOREWORD	5
TABLE OF CONTENTS	7
INTRODUCTION	9
BELIEVE IT	11
THE WORD ETERNAL	14
THE BIBLE	17
"THE WORD OF GOD"	19
THREE QUESTIONS	20
FAITH	20
SECURED FROM WHAT?	23
SATAN	26
SECURITY IN WHAT?	31
UNDER HIS WINGS	34
HOW TO OBTAIN ETERNAL SECURITY	36
WE MUST BE BORN AGAIN	42
HEAD NOT HEART KNOWLEDGE	45
NEW LIFE	46
CAN'T BE CAST AWAY	49
DAVID'S SIN	51
CHASTISEMENT	55
HOLY SPIRIT	56
PROOF OF ETERNAL SECURITY	59
LOVE AND GRACE	61
NO ESCAPE	64
SECURITY	66
NOT BY WORKS	70
KEPT BY GOD	73
REDEEMED	77
ETERNAL SECURITY	79
CONCLUSION	82
SCRIPTURE REFERENCES	85
INDEX	89
ABOUT THE AUTHOR	99

ETERNAL SALVATION

INTRODUCTION

I have no knowledge of the numerous times eternal salvation is taught in the Bible either directly or indirectly. This book only refers to a few. For a person to become a Christian and know without any doubt that he is cleansed from all his sins, past, present, and future, and that he has a free ticket to heaven bought and paid for by the precious Blood of Jesus Christ can only come by faith. "…faith cometh by hearing, and hearing by the word of God." You must know it, believe it, and live by it. God has no pleasure in one who doubts his word. Believing that you have the accurate word of God is the only way you will not pick and choose what you think, desire, accept, and/or what you won't accept. I believe many people today avoid church and/or reading their Bible because they doubt the truth and won't put forth the time and energy to find it. This book was written in an attempt to reveal God's truth in knowing you can trust God's word and know that you have "Eternal Salvation." It is my desire that this book will whet the appetite of those who read it, to study for themselves, and conclude that every word in the King James Bible is absolute truth.

Romans 10:17 So then faith cometh by hearing, and hearing by the word of God.

Hebrews 11:6 But without faith it is impossible to please him: for he that cometh to God must believe that he is, and that he is a rewarder of them that diligently seek him.

Hebrews 10:17 And their sins and iniquities will I remember no more.

Hebrews 10:18 Now where remission of these is, there is no more offering for sin.

BELIEVE IT

The term eternal life or eternal salvation has been and is an essential belief for those who are saved. The term "eternal" means without beginning or end, continuous, perpetual, enduring throughout eternity. Spiros Zodhiates in his book, "The Complete Word Study Dictionary" says: "When referring to eternal life, it means the life which is God's and hence it is not affected by the limitations of time." There are numerous references in the (KJV) Bible referring to "eternal life" and "everlasting life." The problem seems to reside with believing the Bible or adding to or taking away from it. I believe the Bible! It appears to me that those who say you cannot know you have eternal life and those who say you can lose your salvation will not accept the Bible as God's spoken eternal word written by men of God who were moved by the Holy Ghost. Jesus himself said: not "….one jot or one tittle shall no wise pass from the law, till all be fulfilled." A jot and tittle in the Hebrew compared to the English alphabet would be like the crossing of a "t" or the dotting of an "i." Believe it, get saved, and know you have eternal life. God cannot lie!

2 Peter 1:20-21 (KJV) Knowing this first, that no prophecy of the scripture is of any private interpretation. For the prophecy came not in old time by the will of man: but holy men of God spake as they were moved by the Holy Ghost.

2 Timothy 3:16 All scripture is given by inspiration of God, and is profitable for doctrine, for reproof, for correction, for instruction in righteousness:

1 Peter 1:23-25 Being born again, not of corruptible seed, but of incorruptible, by the word of God, which liveth and abideth for ever. For all flesh is as grass, and all the glory of man as the flower of grass. The grass withereth, and the flower thereof falleth away: But the word of the Lord endureth for ever. And this is the word which by the gospel is preached unto you.

Proverbs 30:5 Every word of God is pure: he is a shield unto them that put their trust in him.

Mark 13:31 Heaven and earth shall pass away: but my words shall not pass away.

Hebrews 4:12 For the word of God is quick, and powerful, and sharper than any twoedged sword, piercing even to the dividing asunder of soul and spirit, and of the joints and marrow, and is a discerner of the thoughts and intents of the heart.

Matthew 5:18 For verily I say unto you, Till heaven and earth pass, one jot or one tittle shall in no wise pass from the law, till all be fulfilled.

Titus 1:2 In hope of eternal life, which God, that cannot lie, promised before the world began;

Revelation 22:18-19 For I testify unto every man that heareth the words of the prophecy of this book, If any man shall add unto these things, God shall add unto him the plagues that are written in this book: And if any man shall take away from the words of the book of this prophecy, God shall take away his part out of the book of life, and out of the holy city, and from the things which are written in this book.

THE WORD ETERNAL

It is interesting and imperative to note that the same words eternal and everlasting are also used to define the eternity of hell. Look up also the word "forever." There are some who believe in eternal life, but do not believe in eternal damnation. They believe that a lost person dying without Christ simply is annihilated and exists no longer. Why won't one believe the entire word of God? Eternal means eternal! God's word is truth! It is He who establishes the difference between truth and lies, right and wrong, not you or me. My mother and daddy were divorced when I was two years old. He left my mother and five children in 1936 during the depression. When I grew up I established a friendly relationship with him. He was a Jehovah Witness. He believed that hell was simply a place of total destruction, not eternal punishment. We had many conversations and exchanges of letters concerning hell and many other Bible doctrines. We failed to agree until on one visit to my home we set up a small table with two chairs and a pitcher of tea and two glasses in our back yard. I had my King James Bible and a Strong's Concordance. He had his Bible and several other books. We both had pencil and paper. We studied subjects such as salvation, hell, eternal security, and other topics all day long. We would put a subject at the top of a page and make two columns. On one side we put verses that were very clear. On the other side we put the very few verses which taken alone could be a <u>little</u> obscure. We both agreed that <u>all</u> scripture was <u>true</u>. When we finished there were numerous verses on the clear sides of each subject and only a very few (totally) on the other sides. He was awakened to God's truth, trusted Christ, and was baptized the next Sunday in a Baptist church. Paul writing to Timothy said study the word of God. Many people read books which will profit them very little; but the Bible contains God's words (not man's) which will show those who study it how to be saved, how to please and live for God, and how you can <u>know</u> you have eternal life – God's <u>great</u> <u>gift </u>to undeserving sinners. Could there ever be a greater gift? To God be the glory.

2 Thessalonians 1:9 Who shall be punished with everlasting destruction from the presence of the Lord, and from the glory of his power;

Matthew 25:41, 46 Then shall he say also unto them on the left hand, Depart from me, ye cursed, into everlasting fire, prepared for the devil and his angels:, 46 And these shall go away into everlasting punishment: but the righteous into life eternal.

Jude 7 Even as Sodom and Gomorrha, and the cities about them in like manner, giving themselves over to fornication, and going after strange flesh, are set forth for an example, suffering the vengeance of eternal fire.

Hebrews 6:12 That ye be not slothful, but followers of them who through faith and patience inherit the promises.

Revelation 20:10 And the devil that deceived them was cast into the lake of fire and brimstone, where the beast and the false prophet are, and shall be tormented day and night for ever and ever.

Revelation 14:11 And the smoke of their torment ascendeth up for ever and ever: and they have no rest day nor night, who worship the beast and his image, and whosoever receiveth the mark of his name.

2 Timothy 2:15 Study to shew thyself approved unto God, a workman that needeth not to be ashamed, rightly dividing the word of truth.

THE BIBLE

H.D. Williams is the author of many great books, mostly defending the truth of the King James Bible and repudiating the numerous so-called modern translations. In his book, "The Miracle of Biblical Inspiration," available at "The Old Paths Publications," he states "….that the words that underline the King James Bible English translation are the original perfect words "given by inspiration of God" to "holy men of God" to record. God has providentially superintended the accurate, faithful, verbal, plenary, formal, equivalent translation of the preserved original-languages into the receptor languages of the world so that some translations

ETERNAL SALVATION

can be said to be without translational errors." He goes on to prove that our King James Version of the Bible fits into this classic definition. This Bible contains sixty-six books, written in Hebrew, Aramaic, and Greek by about 40 different authors. They lived over a period of +/-1,600 years. They were written from three different continents. Yet they all complement one another <u>without error</u>. It contains numerous prophesies written long before they occurred which as time passed have proven to be absolutely correct. We can be assured that <u>all</u> prophesies which have not been fulfilled will be as this dispensation draws to a close. Why won't we read the Bible, study it, believe it, and receive eternal salvation? I cannot even dream of any greater physical gift which could ever exist on this earth other than the gift of Jesus Christ himself and knowing without any doubt you have eternal salvation. Most of us in America will let our Bible deteriorate on the shelf while many others in far away places recognize its value and long for the day that they could have their very own Bible. May God help us all. God's word does not change. It endures forever. Nothing can be added or deleted. We should treasure it more than a bag of gold. In it you can find immortality. Pastor D. A. Waite, Th.D., PH.D., editor of "The Defined King James Bible" on page xxiv quotes the following which is an excellent description of the contents of "The Word of God."

"THE WORD OF GOD"

"The Bible contains the mind of God, the state of man, the way of salvation, the doom of sinners, and the happiness of believers.

Its doctrines are holy, its precepts are binding, its histories are true, and its decisions are immutable. Read it to be wise, believe it to be safe, and practice it to be holy. It contains light to direct you, food to support you, and comfort to cheer you. It is the traveler's map, the pilgrim's staff, the pilot's compass, the soldier's sword, and the Christian's charter.

Here paradise is restored, heaven opened and hell disclosed. The Lord Jesus Christ is its grand Object, our good its design, and the glory of God its end. Read it slowly, frequently, and prayerfully. Let it fill the memory, rule the heart, and guide the feet. It is a mine of wealth, a paradise of glory, and a river of pleasure. It is given you in life, will be opened in the judgment, and remembered forever. It involves the highest responsibility, will reward the highest labor, and will condemn all who trifle with its sacred contents."   Author Unknown

Psalm 119:89 LAMED. For ever, O LORD, thy word is settled in heaven.

ETERNAL SALVATION

> ***Psalm 33:4** For the word of the LORD is right; and all his works are done in truth.*
>
> ***Ecclesiastes 3:14** I know that, whatsoever God doeth, it shall be for ever: nothing can be put to it, nor any thing taken from it: and God doeth it, that men should fear before him.*

THREE QUESTIONS

The phrase "eternal security" begs the answer to three questions. First, secured <u>from what,</u> second, "eternal security" <u>in what,</u> and third, how do you <u>obtain it.</u> A cursory study of the (KJV) Bible clearly reveals the answer to all three of these questions.

FAITH

To answer these questions one must put their faith in TRUTH not established by man, but truth established by a holy God. God's word says, "Now faith is the substance of things hoped for, the evidence of things not seen." (Hebrews 11:1) "But without faith it is impossible to please him (God), for he that cometh to God must believe that he is, and that he is a rewarder of them that diligently seek him." (Hebrews 11:6). Faith is believing;

knowing without doubt that something is absolute truth. It matters not that you can't see it, feel it, touch it, smell it, or taste it. You know without any doubt that it is an indestructible fact. We all put faith in our daily lives in many things. Faith that a chair will hold you up; Faith that an airplane will get you to your destination; Faith in your spouse, pastor, and friends; Faith that gravity will keep you from flying off the earth; Faith that your food and water are safe to consume, and the list goes on and on, and on. Why not the Bible, God's holy word? It proves itself to be a supernatural book which could have <u>only</u> been written by a holy God. Faith and truth for eternal security can only be determined and found in the one who can not lie. **Psalm 119:89** "LAMED. For ever, O LORD, thy word is settled in heaven." The one who recorded it, the creator of the universe and life itself cannot lie. He gave us the Bible for our ensamples, our admonition. The author is our holy God. If God the creator says saved people have eternal salvation and it's forever settled you can believe it and be assured that you can't lose it. It is eternal.

1 Corinthians 10:11 Now all these things happened unto them for ensamples: and they are written for our admonition, upon whom the ends of the world are come.

John 3:33 He that hath received his testimony hath set to his seal that God is true.

John 19:35 And he that saw it bare record, and his record is true: and he knoweth that he saith true, that ye might believe.

Romans 3:3-4 For what if some did not believe? shall their unbelief make the faith of God without effect? God forbid: yea, let God be true, but every man a liar; as it is written, That thou mightest be justified in thy sayings, and mightest overcome when thou art judged.

1 John 5:20 And we know that the Son of God is come, and hath given us an understanding, that we may know him that is true, and we are in him that is true, even in his Son Jesus Christ. This is the true God, and eternal life.

ETERNAL SALVATION

SECURED FROM WHAT?

Returning to the three questions: Secured from what? Eternal security in what? and How do you obtain it? First, secured from what? The Bible teaches that the soul that sinneth it shall die. God said let us make man in our image. God's image exists in three persons, but <u>one</u> God. God the father, God the Son, and God the Holy Ghost, a triune God. Now we know that none of us look like God, so what did he mean? We are created in three parts, body, soul, and spirit, a triune man, <u>but</u> only one man. God created man (his body), and breathed into his nostrils and man became a living soul. God even gave him a "helpmeet" (Eve). They were placed in a garden which provided their every need. God communed directly with Adam in the garden. He gave Adam only one direct command telling him he could eat of everything in the garden but one, the tree of knowledge of good and evil. God said the day you eat of that tree you will surely die. Eve was deceived by the lies of Satan and she did eat of the forbidden fruit. She then gave Adam the fruit and he knowingly sinned by disobeying God and eating. But their bodies <u>did not die that day</u>. Adam lived many years after that. So, what died? It was their spirit, the third part of man which could commune with God. To worship God, we must worship him in truth and <u>spirit</u>. Without the Holy Spirit of God living in us in this

Dispensation of Grace we are lost, eternally separated from God, and doomed to spend an eternity in hell. When a person is saved, the Holy Spirit returns and once again they can commune with God. That's eternal salvation.

Ezekiel 18:20a The soul that sinneth, it shall die.

Genesis 1:28 And God blessed them, and God said unto them, Be fruitful, and multiply, and replenish the earth, and subdue it: and have dominion over the fish of the sea, and over the fowl of the air, and over every living thing that moveth upon the earth.

Deuteronomy 6:4 Hear, O Israel: The LORD our God is one LORD:

Genesis 2:7 And the LORD God formed man of the dust of the ground, and breathed into his nostrils the breath of life; and man became a living soul.

Genesis 2:18, 21-25 And the LORD God said, It is not good that the man should be alone; I will make him an help meet for him. [2:21-25] And the LORD God caused a deep sleep to fall upon Adam, and he slept: and he took one of his ribs, and closed up the flesh instead thereof; And the rib, which the LORD God had taken from man, made he a woman, and brought her unto the man. And Adam said, This is now bone of my bones, and flesh of my flesh: she shall be called Woman, because she was taken out of Man. Therefore shall a man leave his father and his mother, and shall cleave unto his wife: and they shall be one flesh. And they were both naked, the man and his wife, and were not ashamed.

Genesis 2:17 But of the tree of the knowledge of good and evil, thou shalt not eat of it: for in the day that thou eatest thereof thou shalt surely die.

John 4:24 God is a Spirit: and they that worship him must worship him in spirit and in truth.

1 Timothy 2:14 And Adam was not deceived, but the woman being deceived was in the transgression.

Genesis 3:4-6 And the serpent said unto the woman, Ye shall not surely die: For God doth know that in the day ye eat thereof, then your eyes shall be opened, and ye shall be as gods, knowing good and evil. And when the woman saw that the tree was good for food, and that it was pleasant to the eyes, and a tree to be desired to make one wise, she took of the fruit thereof, and did eat, and gave also unto her husband with her; and he did eat.

SATAN

The devil (Satan) is real. He will entice you and anyone just as he did Eve. We must beware of his lies and enticements. He will blind the minds of those who believe not. Their final destination WILL be the lake of fire. Eternally damned, separated from God, and tormented for all eternity. He is like a roaring lion, always stalking. His purpose is to entice man into sin and in worshiping him. Sin is rebellion against God. It is wickedness in the sight of God. But we can't blame the devil without accepting our own responsibility. The lust of the flesh, the lust of the eye, and the pride of life have caused us <u>all</u> to sin. "If we say we have no sin, we deceive ourselves and the truth is not in us." (John 1:8) The Bible also says there will be no liars in heaven.

2 Corinthians 4:4 In whom the god of this world hath blinded the minds of them which believe not, lest the light of the glorious gospel of Christ, who is the image of God, should shine unto them.

1 Peter 5:8 Be sober, be vigilant; because your adversary the devil, as a roaring lion, walketh about, seeking whom he may devour:

1 John 2:15-17 Love not the world, neither the things that are in the world. If any man love the world,

the love of the Father is not in him. For all that is in the world, the lust of the flesh, and the lust of the eyes, and the pride of life, is not of the Father, but is of the world. And the world passeth away, and the lust thereof: but he that doeth the will of God abideth for ever.

James 1:14-15 But every man is tempted, when he is drawn away of his own lust, and enticed. Then when lust hath conceived, it bringeth forth sin: and sin, when it is finished, bringeth forth death.

James 4:17 Therefore to him that knoweth to do good, and doeth it not, to him it is sin.

James 2:10 For whosoever shall keep the whole law, and yet offend in one point, he is guilty of all.

Every person who has ever stood on this earth, except Jesus who was God the Son, was, is, or will be a sinner. The Bible teaches us that if we love Jesus we <u>will</u> keep his commandments. Adam

ETERNAL SALVATION

ushered sin into this world and death by sin, so death passed upon all men for all have sinned. The Bible teaches us this is the second death, the lake of fire, eternal damnation, eternally separated from God. If you are not saved now is the time to get saved and have eternal life. When we have eternal salvation we are secured <u>from</u> an everlasting torment in the fire of hell.

> ***Romans 6:23 For the wages of sin is death; but the gift of God is eternal life through Jesus Christ our Lord.***
>
> ***John 1:8 He was not that Light, but was sent to bear witness of that Light.***
>
> ***Romans 5:12 Wherefore, as by one man sin entered into the world, and death by sin; and so death passed upon all men, for that all have sinned:***
>
> ***Revelation 20:10-15 And the devil that deceived them was cast into the lake of fire and brimstone, where the beast and the false prophet are, and shall be tormented***

day and night for ever and ever. And I saw a great white throne, and him that sat on it, from whose face the earth and the heaven fled away; and there was found no place for them. And I saw the dead, small and great, stand before God; and the books were opened: and another book was opened, which is the book of life: and the dead were judged out of those things which were written in the books, according to their works. And the sea gave up the dead which were in it; and death and hell delivered up the dead which were in them: and they were judged every man according to their works. And death and hell were cast into the lake of fire. This is the second death. And whosoever was not found written in the book of life was cast into the lake of fire.

Luke 16:23a "And in hell he lift up his eyes, being in torments..."

SECURITY IN WHAT?

The second question: eternal security in what? Believers in Jesus Christ as their Lord and Savior are destined for a place of perfect happiness. An indescribable place which is being prepared by Jesus himself. Christians will have a new incorruptible body. There will be a new heaven and a new earth free of sin, sickness, aging, pain, and death. A place of eternal joy and happiness. Christians will be like Jesus and will be with him to serve and worship him for all eternity. The Bible does not teach soul sleep, limbo, purgatory, or a do over. It teaches to be absent from the body is to be present with the Lord. Jesus told the repentant thief who died on the cross beside him: "Today shalt thou be with me in paradise." To die is gain for Christians. For them it is a glorious homecoming. They will see and be with all their family, friends, and others who have trusted Christ and proceeded them in their homecoming. But most of all they will see and be with their Lord and Savior Jesus Christ. Heaven is a place that we can't even imagine the beauty and the things which the Lord himself has prepared for all who love Him and have put their trust and faith in Him. Security in what? Security in the arms of Jesus. Eternal security.

1 Corinthians 2:9 But as it is written, Eye hath not seen, nor ear heard, neither have entered into the heart of man, the things which God hath prepared for them that love him.

Philippians 1:23 For I am in a strait betwixt two, having a desire to depart, and to be with Christ; which is far better:

Philippians 3:20-21 For our conversation is in heaven; from whence also we look for the Saviour, the Lord Jesus Christ: Who shall change our vile body, that it may be fashioned like unto his glorious body, according to the working whereby he is able even to subdue all things unto himself.

2 Corinthians 5:1 For we know that if our earthly house of this tabernacle were dissolved, we have a building of God, an house not made with hands, eternal in the heavens.

1 Thessalonians 4:17 Then we which are alive and remain shall be caught up together with them in the clouds, to meet the Lord in the air: and so shall we ever be with the Lord.

John 5:28-29 Marvel not at this: for the hour is coming, in the which all that are in the graves shall hear his voice, And shall come forth; they that have done good, unto the resurrection of life; and they that have done evil, unto the resurrection of damnation.

Revelation 21:1-5 And I saw a new heaven and a new earth: for the first heaven and the first earth were passed away; and there was no more sea. And I John saw the holy city, new Jerusalem, coming down from God out of heaven, prepared as a bride adorned for her husband. And I heard a great voice out of heaven saying, Behold, the tabernacle of God is with men, and he will dwell with them, and they shall be his people, and God himself shall be with them, and be their God. And God shall wipe away all tears from their eyes; and there shall be no more death, neither sorrow, nor crying, neither shall there be any more pain: for the former things are passed away. And he that sat upon the throne said, Behold, I make all things new. And he said unto me, Write: for these words are true and faithful.

2 Corinthians 5:8 We are confident, I say, and willing rather to be absent from the body, and to be present with the Lord.

Luke 23:43 And Jesus said unto him, Verily I say unto thee, To day shalt thou be with me in paradise.

UNDER HIS WINGS

I was recently visiting in a neighborhood on a cold morning. I was driving up a driveway to a house when I saw a sight that brought me to an immediate stop. I saw a large white dog lying on

ETERNAL SALVATION

his stomach on the sunny side of the house. He was resting on his front forearms. What was unusual was that I saw two heads, his head and a cat's head. They were very close, almost touching. On further observation I discovered the cat was cuddled under the dog's chest and two front paws, almost completely covered. The cat's appearance was contentment, safety, comfort, and warmth. The dog appeared to be dominant over the cat with love and protection. What a sight! I just sat there with admiration until they both got up together and moved over to investigate my truck. The both allowed me to pet them. Their love and devotion to one another were undeniable.

    I could not help but remember what Jesus said to the people of Jerusalem. He called them killers, yet he demonstrated his unwavering love by saying how often he wanted to gather them together as a hen gathers her brood under her wings but they would not. To be safe and secure under the wings of Jesus is exactly what Christians have; total eternal security which no one or anything can breach. But many won't believe. We have security in Jesus Christ because He said it! Eternal salvation.

__Matthew 23:37 O Jerusalem, Jerusalem, thou that killest the prophets, and stonest them which are sent unto thee, how often would__

I have gathered thy children together, even as a hen gathereth her chickens under her wings, and ye would not!

Luke 13:34 O Jerusalem, Jerusalem, which killest the prophets, and stonest them that are sent unto thee; how often would I have gathered thy children together, as a hen doth gather her brood under her wings, and ye would not!

HOW TO OBTAIN ETERNAL SECURITY

The third question: How do we obtain eternal security? The Bible teaches that salvation can only be obtained through Jesus Christ. It is a free gift. You can't earn it by good works, and you certainly can't buy it. A saved person becomes a son (or daughter) of God by receiving Jesus Christ as their Lord and Savior. Jesus as I have already said was and is God in the flesh, the third part of our triune God. Since all of us have sinned and come short of the glory God we <u>must</u> have a savior. One who has never sinned. One who will redeem us from our sins. Since we all sin, the only one who can do that is Jesus Christ, God himself. He came to earth as

100% man but retained his sovereignty as 100% God. Jesus came to this earth for <u>one</u> purpose, that is to save sinners. WE CAN'T SAVE OURSELVES! In the sight of God "...all our righteousness is as filthy rags,..." Figuratively speaking, if I stood before the pearly gates of heaven and the door keeper asked "Why should I let you in," and I replied "I went to church." He would say, "One filthy rag." "But I gave my tithe." Two filthy rags. "But I lived good and kept the ten commandments...." more filthy rags. "But why are all my good works like filthy rags?" Because if on a balance scale we put all the good works we have ever accomplished on one side, and one drop of the blood of Jesus Christ which he shed for us on the other, the scale would forever be weighted down with the Blood of Jesus Christ. We are redeemed <u>only</u> by the precious Blood of Jesus Christ. The door keeper would say, "Depart from here into an everlasting hell prepared for the devil and his angels." The Bible teaches that without the shedding of blood there is no remission for our sins, not just any blood, but blood from the only sinless one, God in the flesh. He suffered an agonizing death which mortal man can't comprehend to save us. He was innocent. No fault was found in Him. Yet he was despised and rejected. They spat on him, buffeted him, placed a crown of thorns on his head, beat his head with a rod, scourged him, mocked him, and crucified him by nailing him to a cross. His appearance was so disfigured by all the torture and pain that he was unrecognizable. The last thing he said before giving up his life was, "It is finished." He paid the price in full. We either accept Jesus and his blood for full payment for our sins and be saved or, by choice, we will die in our sins and spend eternity in hell.

Jesus' body was taken down from the cross and placed in a tomb. After three days and three nights he came out of the tomb and now sits on the right hand of God the Father interceding for us before a holy God. Proof that his testimony is true.

> ***Ephesians 2:8-9 For by grace are ye saved through faith; and that not of yourselves: it is the gift of God: Not of works, lest any man should boast.***
>
> ***John 1:12 But as many as received him, to them gave he power to become the sons of God, even to them that believe on his name:***
>
> ***Acts 4:12 Neither is there salvation in any other: for there is none other name under heaven***

given among men, whereby we must be saved.

John 14:6 Jesus saith unto him, I am the way, the truth, and the life: no man cometh unto the Father, but by me.

Romans 3:23 For all have sinned, and come short of the glory of God;

1 Timothy 1:15 This is a faithful saying, and worthy of all acceptation, that Christ Jesus came into the world to save sinners; of whom I am chief.

John 3:18 He that believeth on him is not condemned: but he that believeth not is condemned already, because he hath not believed in the name of the only begotten Son of God.

John 19:3, 6 And said, Hail, King of the Jews! and they smote him with their hands. [6] When the chief priests therefore and officers

ETERNAL SALVATION

saw him, they cried out, saying, Crucify him, crucify him. Pilate saith unto them, Take ye him, and crucify him: for I find no fault in him.

John 19:17-18 And he bearing his cross went forth into a place called the place of a skull, which is called in the Hebrew Golgotha: Where they crucified him, and two other with him, on either side one, and Jesus in the midst.

Isaiah 52:14 As many were astonied at thee; his visage was so marred more than any man, and his form more than the sons of men:

Isaiah 53:3-12 He is despised and rejected of men; a man of sorrows, and acquainted with grief: and we hid as it were our faces from him; he was despised, and we esteemed him not. Surely he hath borne our griefs, and carried our sorrows: yet we did esteem him stricken, smitten of God, and afflicted. But he was wounded for our transgressions, he was bruised for our iniquities: the chastisement of our peace was upon him; and with his stripes we are healed. All we like sheep have gone astray; we have turned every one to his own way; and the LORD hath laid on him the iniquity of us all. He was oppressed, and he was afflicted, yet he opened not his mouth: he is brought as a lamb to the slaughter, and as a sheep before her shearers is dumb, so he openeth not his mouth. He was taken from prison and from judgment: and who shall declare his generation? for he was cut off out of the land of the living: for the transgression of my people was he stricken. And he made his grave with the wicked, and with the rich in his death; because he had done no violence, neither was any deceit in his mouth. Yet it pleased the LORD to bruise him; he hath put him to grief: when thou shalt make his soul an offering for sin, he shall see his seed, he shall prolong his days, and the pleasure of the LORD shall prosper in his hand. He shall see of the travail of his soul, and shall be satisfied: by his knowledge shall my righteous servant justify many; for he shall bear their iniquities. Therefore will I divide him a portion with the great, and he shall divide the spoil with the strong; because he hath poured out his soul unto death: and he was numbered with the transgressors; and he bare the sin of many, and made intercession for the transgressors.

WE MUST BE BORN AGAIN

We must be born again to be saved. Nicodemus, in John Chapter three, was a Pharisee. They believed they were the separated ones, very religious, but not saved. They believed separation from other sinners was the way to please God. Jesus called Nicodemus a "ruler," a high official in his religious group. He also called him a "master" which means teacher. He taught religion and was probably considered righteous in man's sight. But he came to Jesus lost on his way to hell. Jesus was telling Nicodemus that his religion and good works would not save him. <u>He MUST be born again</u>. He said, "For God so loved the world that he gave his only begotten Son, that whosoever believeth in him should not perish but have everlasting life." (*John 3:16*) Everlasting salvation.

> **John 3:3 Jesus answered and said unto him, Verily, verily, I say unto thee, Except a man be born again, he cannot see the kingdom of God.**

> **Ephesians 2:8-9 For by grace are ye saved through faith; and that not of yourselves: it is the gift of God: Not of works, lest any man should boast.**

The apostles taught that we have redemption through the blood of Jesus Christ, the forgiveness of sins according to the riches of his grace. In whom we trusted after hearing, believing, and receiving that Christ died for our sins, was buried, and rose again the third day. We must be born again!

> **Ephesians 1:7, 13 In whom we have redemption through his blood, the forgiveness of sins, according to**

the riches of his grace; [13] In whom ye also trusted, after that ye heard the word of truth, the gospel of your salvation: in whom also after that ye believed, ye were sealed with that holy Spirit of promise,

1 Corinthians 15:1-4 Moreover, brethren, I declare unto you the gospel which I preached unto you, which also ye have received, and wherein ye stand; By which also ye are saved, if ye keep in memory what I preached unto you, unless ye have believed in vain. For I delivered unto you first of all that which I also received, how that Christ died for our sins according to the scriptures; And that he was buried, and that he rose again the third day according to the scriptures:

Romans 8:11 But if the Spirit of him that raised up Jesus from the dead dwell in you, he that raised up Christ from the dead shall also quicken your mortal bodies by his Spirit that dwelleth in you.

HEAD NOT HEART KNOWLEDGE

There are many who have a head knowledge of Christ but not a heart knowledge. In other words, they believe that Jesus existed and actually died for their sins, but they have never <u>trusted</u> him with their <u>heart</u>. God says we must repent, believe, and call on Jesus to be saved. Repentance is changing one's mind by turning away from our life of sin and earnestly seeking a positive relationship with God. The Bible says: "That if thou shalt confess with the mouth the Lord Jesus, and shalt believe in thine heart that God hath raised him from the dead, thou shalt be saved. For with the heart man believeth unto righteousness; and with the mouth confession is made unto salvation." *(Romans 10:9, 10)* Have you really repented, believed, and called on Jesus to save you? If not, do it now! We will all have <u>eternal security</u> in either heaven or hell. The choice is ours and ours alone. Jesus saves! Eternal security is eternal salvation.

2 Peter 3:9 The Lord is not slack concerning his promise, as some men count slackness; but is longsuffering to us-ward, not willing that any should perish, but that all should come to repentance.

> *John 3:18 He that believeth on him is not condemned: but he that believeth not is condemned already, because he hath not believed in the name of the only begotten Son of God.*

NEW LIFE

A saved person has a new life, old things are passed away, all things become new. We can no longer <u>live</u> in habitual sin and get away with it. It must be confessed for forgiveness. If not, we will bring chastisement upon ourselves. Be assured that a Christian life includes trials and tribulations, but also be assured that you will have peace and joy beyond our ability to describe. Jesus writing to little children (immature Christians) said "sin not," but if you do, and we all do, we have an advocate with the Father, Jesus Christ the righteous, and he is the propitiation for our sins and also for the sins of the whole world. "If we say that we have no sin we deceive ourselves, and the truth is not in us." (*I John 1:8*) The good news is if we confess our sins, God in his mercy forgives us and cleanses us from all unrighteousness. Advocate means legal advisor, like a lawyer who will plead your case, standing between you and your accuser, the devil. Propitiation means atonement, the payment with the Blood of Jesus Christ for our sins. In other words, when we sin our accuser, Satan, must go through Jesus to reach our Heavenly Father. Jesus would say something like this. Not so fast, I can't even remember that sin. Nevertheless, I paid for them all with my own Blood.

2 Corinthians 5:17 Therefore if any man be in Christ, he is a new creature: old things are passed away; behold, all things are become new.

1 John 1:9 If we confess our sins, he is faithful and just to forgive us our sins, and to cleanse us from all unrighteousness.

1 John 2:1-2 My little children, these things write I unto you, that ye sin not. And if any man sin, we have an advocate with the Father, Jesus Christ the righteous: And he is the propitiation for our sins: and not for ours only, but also for the sins of the whole world.

1 John 2:3-4 And hereby we do know that we know him, if we keep his commandments. He that saith, I

ETERNAL SALVATION

know him, and keepeth not his commandments, is a liar, and the truth is not in him.

Hebrews 12:5-8, 11 And ye have forgotten the exhortation which speaketh unto you as unto children, My son, despise not thou the chastening of the Lord, nor faint when thou art rebuked of him: For whom the Lord loveth he chasteneth, and scourgeth every son whom he receiveth. If ye endure chastening, God dealeth with you as with sons; for what son is he whom the father chasteneth not? But if ye be without chastisement, whereof all are partakers, then are ye bastards, and not sons. [11] Now no chastening for the present seemeth to be joyous, but grievous: nevertheless afterward it yieldeth the peaceable fruit of righteousness unto them which are exercised thereby.

Philippians 4:7 And the peace of God, which passeth all

understanding, shall keep your hearts and minds through Christ Jesus.

CAN'T BE CAST AWAY

We Christians should be eternally grateful that God <u>doesn't</u> cast us away when we sin. If he did heaven would be empty except for angels. An illustration I sometimes use on visitation concerning eternal security is a variation of the following: When you were little your mother would give you a commandment like don't play in the street, but you did anyway. What if you went to your mother and said, "Mother you gave me a commandment and I broke it. Will you forgive me?" What would your mother do? Would she forgive you being grateful that you are at last demonstrating some maturity, or would she pack your clothes and throw you out of the house? Keep in mind that since you are immature you will get in the street again, but she knows that with your repentant heart it won't be long before you would be only playing in the yard. She would forgive you! God would certainly do no less! But what if every time she let you go play you ran to the street, what would she do? Because she loves you, she would punish you in an attempt to make you learn that the street is dangerous, and you must learn. God for certain would do no less. We sometimes chasten for our own pleasure, but

ETERNAL SALVATION

God chastens us for our profit. To improve our behavior. No Christian can escape God's chastening. He said "...if ye be without chastisement whereof all are partakers, then are ye bastards, and not sons."

Hebrews 12:5b-11 My son, despise not thou the chastening of the Lord, nor faint when thou art rebuked of him: For whom the Lord loveth he chasteneth, and scourgeth every son whom he receiveth. If ye endure chastening, God dealeth with you as with sons; for what son is he whom the father chasteneth not? But if ye be without chastisement, whereof all are partakers, then are ye bastards, and not sons. Furthermore we have had fathers of our flesh which corrected us, and we gave them reverence: shall we not much rather be in subjection unto the Father of spirits, and live? For they verily for a few days chastened us after their own pleasure; but he for our profit, that we might be partakers of his holiness. Now no chastening for the present seemeth to be joyous, but grievous: nevertheless afterward it yieldeth the peaceable fruit of righteousness unto them which are exercised thereby.

1 John 1:9 If we confess our sins, he is faithful and just to forgive us our sins, and to cleanse us from all unrighteousness.

1 John 3:1 Behold, what manner of love the Father hath bestowed upon us, that we should be called the sons of God: therefore the world knoweth us not, because it knew him not. John 6:37 All that the Father giveth me shall come to me; and him that cometh to me I will in no wise cast out.

DAVID'S SIN

Keep in mind King David sinned. He committed adultery, murder, and I'm sure other sins, but he was a man after God's own heart. He knew how to repent, confess his sins, and get back into fellowship with God. God did not cast him away, but he was thoroughly chastened. God took

David's first son home to heaven while a young baby. God allowed another son Absalom to attempt to take away his kingdom. David was chastened but <u>not cast</u> out.

> *2 Samuel 11:3-5 And David sent and inquired after the woman. And one said, Is not this Bathsheba, the daughter of Eliam, the wife of Uriah the Hittite? And David sent messengers, and took her; and she came in unto him, and he lay with her; for she was purified from her uncleanness: and she returned unto her house. And the woman conceived, and sent and told David, and said, I am with child.*

> *2 Samuel 11:15 And he wrote in the letter, saying, Set ye Uriah in the forefront of the hottest battle, and retire ye from him, that he may be smitten, and die.*

> *2 Samuel 11:26-27 And when the wife of Uriah heard that Uriah her husband was dead, she mourned for her husband. And when the mourning was past, David*

sent and fetched her to his house, and she became his wife, and bare him a son. But the thing that David had done displeased the LORD.

2 Samuel 12:9-14 Wherefore hast thou despised the commandment of the LORD, to do evil in his sight? thou hast killed Uriah the Hittite with the sword, and hast taken his wife to be thy wife, and hast slain him with the sword of the children of Ammon. Now therefore the sword shall never depart from thine house; because thou hast despised me, and hast taken the wife of Uriah the Hittite to be thy wife. Thus saith the LORD, Behold, I will raise up evil against thee out of thine own house, and I will take thy wives before thine eyes, and give them unto thy neighbour, and he shall lie with thy wives in the sight of this sun. For thou didst it secretly: but I will do this thing before all Israel, and before the sun. And David said unto Nathan, I have sinned against the LORD. And Nathan said unto David, The LORD also hath put away thy sin; thou shalt not die. Howbeit, because by this deed thou hast given great occasion to the enemies of the LORD to blaspheme, the child also that is born unto thee shall surely die.

***2 Samuel 15:13-14** And there came a messenger to David, saying, The hearts of the men of Israel are after Absalom. And David said unto all his servants that were with him at Jerusalem, Arise, and let us flee; for we shall not else escape from Absalom: make speed to depart, lest he overtake us suddenly, and bring evil upon us, and smite the city with the edge of the sword.*

Psalm 51:1-3, 12 *To the chief Musician, A Psalm of David, when Nathan the prophet came unto him, after he had gone in to Bath-sheba.* **Have mercy upon me, O God, according to thy lovingkindness: according unto the**

multitude of thy tender mercies blot out my transgressions. Wash me throughly from mine iniquity, and cleanse me from my sin. For I acknowledge my transgressions: and my sin is ever before me. [12] Restore unto me the joy of thy salvation; and uphold me with thy free spirit.

CHASTISEMENT

Getting back to my illustration, what if every time your mother opened the door you ran to play in the street. Your mother would learn that you can't be trusted and she would keep you as close to her as she could. God will do no less. Your mother loves you and you will always be her child. Some of God's chastisement is described as weak, sickly, and many sleep. Sleep here means death. Death in the body, taken to heaven early. Just like a good mother God will want you in a position to be by his side. God could take you home early to keep you out of trouble. A saved person can never be lost. What if a professing Christian habitually lives in sin and is not chastened by God. The answer is they are a bastard and not a son. They lie and are not saved! God is not their father, the devil is.

1 Corinthians 11:30 For this cause many are weak and sickly among you, and many sleep.

1 John 5:12 He that hath the Son hath life; and he that hath not the Son of God hath not life.

John 8:44-45 Ye are of your father the devil, and the lusts of your father ye will do. He was a murderer from the beginning, and abode not in the truth, because there is no truth in him. When he speaketh a lie, he speaketh of his own: for he is a liar, and the father of it. And because I tell you the truth, ye believe me not.

HOLY SPIRIT

The Holy Spirit is the third person of our triune God. In the Dispensation of Grace when we receive Jesus as our Lord and Savior the Holy Spirit immediately indwells our body. He will be our conscience. He will guide us into all truth. We will recognize sin and God's will for our life. The Holy Spirit was initially lost by Adam. He returns only when we are saved. In this Dispensation of Grace to worship God, we "...must worship him in spirit and in truth." If we have not the Spirit of God living in us, we are lost on our way to an eternal hell.

1 Corinthians 6:19 What? know ye not that your body is the temple of the Holy Ghost which is in you, which ye have of God, and ye are not your own?

John 16:7-8 Nevertheless I tell you the truth; It is expedient for you that I go away: for if I go not away, the Comforter will not come unto you; but if I depart, I will send him unto you. And when he is come, he will reprove the world of sin, and of righteousness, and of judgment:

John 14:15-17, 26 If ye love me, keep my commandments. And I will pray the Father, and he shall give you another Comforter, that he may abide with you for ever; Even the Spirit of truth; whom the world cannot receive, because it seeth him not, neither knoweth him: but ye know him; for he dwelleth with you, and shall be in you. [26] But the Comforter, which is the Holy Ghost, whom the Father will send in my name, he shall teach you all things, and bring all things to your remembrance, whatsoever I have said unto you.

John 4:23-24 But the hour cometh, and now is, when the true worshippers shall worship the Father in spirit and in truth: for the Father seeketh such to worship him. God is a Spirit: and they that worship him must worship him in spirit and in truth.

Romans 8:5-11 For they that are after the flesh do mind the things of the flesh; but they that are after the Spirit the things of the Spirit. For to be carnally minded is death; but to be spiritually minded is life and peace. Because the carnal mind is enmity against God: for it is not subject to the law of God, neither indeed can be. So then they that are in the flesh cannot please

God. But ye are not in the flesh, but in the Spirit, if so be that the Spirit of God dwell in you. Now if any man have not the Spirit of Christ, he is none of his. And if Christ be in you, the body is dead because of sin; but the Spirit is life because of righteousness. But if the Spirit of him that raised up Jesus from the dead dwell in you, he that raised up Christ from the dead shall also quicken your mortal bodies by his Spirit that dwelleth in you.

PROOF OF ETERNAL SECURITY

It is a frightening thought to believe a saved person can lose their salvation or never be assured they do have ETERNAL SALVATION. There are many, many verses in the Bible that confirm, without a smidgen of doubt, that eternal salvation is an indisputable fact. I ask the reader to trust God's word. He cannot lie. When I go door knocking, and it appears appropriate, I give a simple illustration to help demonstrate faith. The words faith and believe are closely related in the Bible. Faith means firm persuasion, conviction based upon hearing, trust. Whereas believe means to be persuaded of, to place confidence in, to trust,

ETERNAL SALVATION

to place reliance upon. (Definitions taken from "An Expository Dictionary of Bible Words" by W. E. Vine.) Since these words basically have the same meaning I believe the following illustration is appropriate. In this illustration I'm referring to faith and believing in the Word of God. I will sometimes ask a person to picture themselves as a little child playing in the yard. Their mother comes to the door and calls to the child that supper is ready and closes the door to keep the dog out. I say to the child, "Where are you going?" The child would answer, "I'm going to supper or to eat." I would then say, "Your mother is the biggest liar in the state of Georgia. There is no food in the house." Who would you believe? Their reply. "My mother." I would then say, "Do you see any food?" They would reply, "No." I would say, "That proves your mother is a liar." Who would you believe? Again, "My mother." I would say, "Are you hungry?" The child would say, "No." I would say, "That proves your mother to be a liar." I would then say, "It doesn't matter if you can't see it, touch it, smell it, or whether or not you're hungry. Your mother said supper is ready. All you have to do is believe it, go into the house and eat. Your mother would never lie about something as important to your well-being as food." I would use the same illustration and ask them if Jesus came to the door and they knew it really was Jesus and he said come to supper and you can eat, and I said

Jesus was a liar. There is no food in the house. Would you believe me or Jesus? Their reply would be Jesus. I would reply if Jesus won't lie about your supper, would he lie about your eternal soul? Of course not! He said, *"For God so loved the world that he gave his only begotten Son, that whosoever believeth in him should not perish but have everlasting life."* (*John 3:16*) Would God lie about eternal life? No, he would tell you the absolute truth, leaving no room for doubt. Eternal salvation.

John 3:15 That whosoever believeth in him should not perish, but have eternal life.

John 3:36 He that believeth on the Son hath everlasting life: and he that believeth not the Son shall not see life; but the wrath of God abideth on him.

LOVE AND GRACE

God's love for us is far beyond our ability to describe or totally understand. He allowed his son Jesus to suffer and shed his blood to save undeserving sinners like you and me. Since God won't tolerate sin in heaven, he would have been justified to let all of us die in our sin and end up in hell. But by his grace he provided one, and only one, way for us to shed our sin and have an eternal home in heaven. That way is by grace through faith in His Son Jesus Christ. That's GRACE. Grace can be defined as an underserving eternal love for us in spite of our rebellion and sins against a holy God or an undeserving free gift. That gift is eternal life which has an infinite value. Human words will never be adequate to describe true meaning of GOD'S LOVE AND GRACE. I have tried to define love and grace but I can't. The best definition I have read is the third verse of the song written by Frederick M. Lehman, "The Love of God," recorded on page 188 of the song book titled "Soul Stirring Songs and Hymns" published by the "Sword of the Lord." That verse is quoted as follows:

> "Could we with ink the ocean fill, and were the skies of parchment made,
> Were ev'ry stalk on earth a quill, And ev'ry man a scribe by trade;
> To write the love of God above Would drain the ocean dry;
> Nor could the scroll contain the whole, Tho' stretched from sky to sky.
> O love of god, how rich and pure! How measureless and strong!
> It shall forever more endure, The saints' and angels' song."

ETERNAL SALVATION

What a gift! All we have to do is just believe. In this case believe, trust, and receive. Any gift given, if it is truly a gift, cannot be reclaimed. It belongs entirely to the receiver. In this case it has such an infinite value no one would give it up assuming they could. The grace of God is not in any way connected to any merit which we may have done. It is God offering man the greatest gift that anyone could ever possess with no strings attached. It is a free gift. It is eternal life ready for everyone. This gift is in total conflict with works. God gives us a free choice: receive his gift of grace or stay in our sinful lost state. We have eternal salvation or we will have an eternal fiery hell.

Romans 8:38-39 For I am persuaded, that neither death, nor life, nor angels, nor principalities, nor powers, nor things present, nor things to come, Nor height, nor depth, nor any other creature, shall be able to separate us from the love of God, which is in Christ Jesus our Lord.

Romans 6:16-18 Know ye not, that to whom ye yield yourselves servants to obey, his servants ye are to whom ye obey; whether of sin unto death, or of obedience unto righteousness? But God be thanked, that ye were the servants of sin, but ye have obeyed from the heart that form of doctrine which was delivered you. Being then made free from sin, ye became the servants of righteousness.

Romans 5:21 That as sin hath reigned unto death, even so might grace reign through righteousness unto eternal life by Jesus Christ our Lord.

Ephesians 2:8-9 For by grace are ye saved through faith; and that not of yourselves: it is the gift of God: Not of works, lest any man should boast.

NO ESCAPE

No one can escape the Word of God. It is absolute truth which can never be altered or changed. It is forever settled in heaven. Have you ever worked for someone and had an agreement that your wages would be so much, and after you fulfilled your agreement they reneged or reduced your wages? I have. Man will and does lie; but not God; he can't lie. If he says that the wages of sin is death (the second death in the lake of fire) you had better believe it. You can hide under a rock, hide yourself in the deepest jungle. or go to another planet. It won't matter. God's Word will always be there and you will receive your just wages.

> **Romans 5:12 Wherefore, as by one man sin entered into the world, and death by sin; and so death passed upon all men, for that all have sinned:**

> **Romans 6:23 For the wages of sin is death; but the gift of God is eternal life through Jesus Christ our Lord.**

If God says he loves us, shed His Blood, and died for our sins and IF we believe it, trust it, and ask Him to save us He will. You will never escape that promise even if you tried. God cannot lie. Eternal security.

> **Romans 5:8-9 But God commendeth his love toward us, in that, while we were yet sinners, Christ died for us. Much more then,**

ETERNAL SALVATION

being now justified by his blood, we shall be saved from wrath through him.

John 1:12 But as many as received him, to them gave he power to become the sons of God, even to them that believe on his name:

Acts 4:12 Neither is there salvation in any other: for there is none other name under heaven given among men, whereby we must be saved.

SECURITY

When a person is truly saved he becomes a new creature. He becomes an heir of God and a joint heir with Jesus Christ. He becomes a member of God's family. God is his Father. <u>Nothing</u> can separate him from the love of Christ. We are sealed by the Holy Spirit. When total security is required, man places a seal on that item. If the seal is broken the goods become tampered with, contaminated, and in many cases useless. It is a crime to break the seal. If man needs more security he would also have a guard. Our guard is the third person of our triune God, the Holy Spirit.

II Corinthians 1:22 says we are not only sealed we have the "earnest of the Spirit in our hearts." "Earnest" here means a pledge given in advance. Like a down payment on a contract or agreement with someone. <u>No one</u> can get by the Holy Spirit to break the seal, not even Satan himself. We've been purchased with the precious Blood of Jesus Christ. God has sealed a contract with us which says: Trust Jesus and you have eternal life. That's security, Eternal Security. That's Eternal salvation!

2 Corinthians 5:17 Therefore if any man be in Christ, he is a new creature: old things are passed away; behold, all things are become new.

Romans 8:35, 38, 39 Who shall separate us from the love of Christ? shall tribulation, or distress, or persecution, or famine, or nakedness, or peril, or sword? [38] For I am persuaded, that neither death, nor life, nor angels, nor principalities, nor powers, nor things present, nor things to come, [39] Nor height, nor depth, nor any other creature, shall be able to

separate us from the love of God, which is in Christ Jesus our Lord.

2 Corinthians 1:22 Who hath also sealed us, and given the earnest of the Spirit in our hearts.

Ephesians 1:7, 13, 14 In whom we have redemption through his blood, the forgiveness of sins, according to the riches of his grace; [13] In whom ye also trusted, after that ye heard the word of truth, the gospel of your salvation: in whom also after that ye believed, ye were sealed with that holy Spirit of promise, [14] Which is the earnest of our inheritance until the redemption of the purchased possession, unto the praise of his glory.

Some people say that's all well and good, but God Himself can toss you away. If so, that would make God a liar and God can't lie. Jesus, God the Son, said: All that come to him "...I will no wise cast out." It is the Father's will that "...I should lose nothing, but should raise it up again at the last day." That's everlasting life. That's security. That's Eternal salvation.

ETERNAL SALVATION

John 6:37, 39-40 All that the Father giveth me shall come to me; and him that cometh to me I will in no wise cast out. [39] And this is the Father's will which hath sent me, that of all which he hath given me I should lose nothing, but should raise it up again at the last day. [40] And this is the will of him that sent me, that every one which seeth the Son, and believeth on him, may have everlasting life: and I will raise him up at the last day.

Some people say that's all well and good but Jesus Himself can toss you away. If so, that would make Jesus a liar, and Jesus can't lie. Jesus said my sheep (followers of Christ, saved people) hear my voice and I give them <u>eternal life</u>, they shall <u>never</u> perish, neither shall any man pluck them out of my hand. He concludes by saying His Father is greater than all "...and no man is able to pluck them out of my Father's hand." Eternal security. Eternal salvation.

John 10:26-29 But ye believe not, because ye are not of my sheep, as I said unto you. My sheep hear my voice, and I know them, and they follow me: And I give unto them eternal life; and they shall never perish, neither shall any man pluck them out of my hand. My Father, which gave them me, is greater than all; and no man is able to pluck them out of my Father's hand.

NOT BY WORKS

If man could be lost by sin after he is saved, then his salvation would be by works and not by faith in the precious incorruptible Blood of Jesus Christ. Jesus said silver, gold, and corruptible things can't save you nor can your vain conversations (behavior, the way you live) save you, only by the Blood. If you could lose your salvation then ALL would be lost for we are all sinners. The Bible says: "There is none righteous, no not one." "For all have sinned and come short of the glory of God." Most of us think we're not just good, but we're very good. That is a lie perpetrated by the devil. When we say we have not sinned we deceive ourselves, the truth is not in us, and we make God out to be a liar. All of us are sinners. A lawyer asked Jesus the question saying, "What shall I do to inherit eternal life?" Jesus told him to love the Lord thy God with all thy soul, strength, and mind and thy neighbor as thyself. Sounds so simple but <u>no one</u> can live that good. If we could, we would not only act like Jesus, we would be Jesus. Even on our death bed we will probably sin by saying: "Why me Lord?" Also, many evil thoughts will probably pass through our mind. That's sin! We cannot live good enough to earn even a peanut toward the price of a ticket to heaven. Jesus <u>paid</u> it all. We either are saved by the grace of God through faith in Jesus or we are NOT SAVED.

> **1 Peter 1:18-19 Forasmuch as ye know that ye were not redeemed with corruptible things, as silver and gold, from your vain conversation received by tradition from your fathers; But with the precious blood of Christ, as of a lamb without blemish and without spot:**

> **Ephesians 2:8-9 For by grace are ye saved through faith; and that not of yourselves: it is the gift of God: Not of works, lest any man should boast.**

> **Romans 3:10 As it is written, There is none righteous, no, not one:**

Romans 3:23 For all have sinned, and come short of the glory of God;

1 John 1:8 If we say that we have no sin, we deceive ourselves, and the truth is not in us.

1 John 1:10 If we say that we have not sinned, we make him a liar, and his word is not in us.

1 John 2:23 Whosoever denieth the Son, the same hath not the Father: [but] he that acknowledgeth the Son hath the Father also.

Romans 3:28 Therefore we conclude that a man is justified by faith without the deeds of the law.

Luke 10:25, 27 And, behold, a certain lawyer stood up, and tempted him, saying, Master, what shall I do to inherit eternal life? [27] And he answering said, Thou shalt love the Lord thy God with all thy heart, and with all thy soul, and with all thy strength, and with all thy mind; and thy neighbour as thyself.

Titus 3:5 Not by works of righteousness which we have done, but according to his mercy he saved us, by the washing of regeneration, and renewing of the Holy Ghost;

KEPT BY GOD

When you were young and close to any danger such as falling off a cliff, close to a fire, or any dangerous place, your mother or father would grab you by the hand to keep you from falling. As a Christian we have God as our Father. His strength is infinite. He will not let you fall. When He says He will keep you from falling and present you faultless before his presence of his glory you can believe it. No one else could ever make such a claim. It's done; it's over. It is an undeniable truth. That's Eternal salvation.

Jude 24-25 Now unto him that is able to keep you from falling, and to present you faultless before the presence of his glory with exceeding joy, To the only wise God our Saviour, be glory and majesty, dominion and power, both now and ever. Amen.

Romans 3:4 God forbid: yea, let God be true, but every man a liar; as it is written, That thou mightest be justified in thy sayings, and mightest overcome when thou art judged.

Have you ever seen a hen gathering her little chicks under her wings in a rain or any sign of danger? She covers them with her wings for their protection. She will protect them by fighting an enemy with her wings, feet and beak. She knows the only protection her chicks have is her. If they dared to go out, they could lose the warmth and be vulnerable to all the dangers the world offers. Jesus used the illustration of a hen protecting her young to demonstrate his love and protection to his flock. He said many times he wanted to protect his people under his wings, but they would not. They would not put their trust in him. They wanted to do everything their way. Those who choose not to trust in Jesus are lost in their sins. Those who choose the protection of Jesus are safe and secure under his wings. Kept by God himself. Eternal security.

Luke 13:34 O Jerusalem, Jerusalem, which killest the prophets, and stonest them that are sent unto thee; how often would I have gathered thy children together, as a hen doth gather her brood under her wings, and ye would not!

Psalm 91:4-5 He shall cover thee with his feathers, and under his wings shalt thou trust: his truth shall be thy shield and buckler. Thou shalt not be afraid for the terror by night; nor for the arrow that flieth by day;

Psalm 91:2 I will say of the LORD, He is my refuge and my fortress: my God; in him will I trust.

Paul under the guidance of the Holy Spirit taught that our Lord and Savior Jesus Christ abolished death and brought life and immortality to light through the gospel, Jesus' death, burial, and resurrection. Paul knew that his dedication and devotion as a preacher, apostle, and teacher would bring him much suffering and many painful hardships. Yet he committed himself to Jesus being persuaded that he is kept by God eternally. Eternal salvation.

1 Corinthians 15:1-4 Moreover, brethren, I declare unto you the gospel which I preached unto you, which also ye have received, and wherein ye stand; By which also ye are saved, if ye keep in memory what I preached unto you, unless ye have believed in vain. For I delivered unto you first of all that which I also received, how that Christ died for our sins according to the scriptures; And that he was buried, and that he rose again the third day according to the scriptures:

2 Timothy 1:10-12 But is now made manifest by the appearing of our Saviour Jesus Christ, who hath abolished death, and hath brought life and immortality to light through the gospel: Whereunto I am appointed a preacher, and an apostle, and a teacher of the Gentiles. For the which cause I also suffer these things: nevertheless I am not ashamed: for I know whom I have believed, and am persuaded that he is able to keep that which I have committed unto him against that day.

REDEEMED

Isaiah said all of us are like sheep which have gone astray. We all want to do our own thing. We are all sinners; but Jesus paid for our sin on the cross of Calvary. "...the Lord hath laid on him (Jesus) the iniquity of us all." He was made an offering for our sin. He paid the price (redeemed) with his blood. We can't redeem ourselves, not even with silver and gold. All our wealth is corruptible things, but not the Blood of Christ. It is incorruptible. Many people believe they are okay. After all they do the best they can. They try to live by the law written in the Bible. They do good works. They don't realize they are cursed because no one can keep all the law. No one! Failure is sin! Christ redeemed us from that curse by becoming a curse for us. We are bought and paid for. All we have to do is accept the payment. REDEEMED BY THE BLOOD OR NOT REDEEMED. SECURED OR NOT SECURED. ETERNALLY SAVED OR ETERNITY LOST.

Isaiah 53:6 All we like sheep have gone astray; we have turned every one to his own way; and the LORD hath laid on him the iniquity of us all.

Isaiah 53:10 Yet it pleased the LORD to bruise him; he hath put him to grief: when thou shalt make his soul an offering for sin, he shall see his seed, he shall prolong his days, and the pleasure of the LORD shall prosper in his hand.

Isaiah 59:12, 20 For our transgressions are multiplied before thee, and our sins testify against us: for our transgressions are with us; and as for our iniquities, we know them; [20] And the Redeemer shall come to Zion, and unto them that turn from transgression in Jacob, saith the LORD.

1 Peter 1:18 Forasmuch as ye know that ye were not redeemed with corruptible things, as silver and gold, from your vain conversation received by tradition from your fathers;

Galatians 3:10-11,13 For as many as are of the works of the law are under the curse: for it is written, Cursed is every one that continueth not in all things which are written in the book of the law to do them. But that no man is justified by the law in the sight of God, it is evident: for, The just shall live by faith. [13] Christ hath redeemed us from the curse of the law, being made a curse for us: for it is written, Cursed is every one that hangeth on a tree:

ETERNAL SECURITY

The apostle John who followed Jesus, was taught by him, and saw him alive after his death and burial. He testified in his epistle I John Chapter 5 over and over how to be saved and <u>know it</u>. For example, in verse:

1 John 5:1 Whosoever believeth that Jesus is the Christ is born of God: and every one that

ETERNAL SALVATION

loveth him that begat loveth him also that is begotten of him.

5:1 Whosoever (that means everyone) that believeth Jesus is the Christ is born of God. They have become members of God's family, on their way to be with our Lord and Savior Jesus Christ. (Eternal salvation)

1 John 5:4-5 For whatsoever is born of God overcometh the world: and this is the victory that overcometh the world, even our faith. Who is he that overcometh the world, but he that believeth that Jesus is the Son of God?

5:4 Whatsoever is born of God overcometh the world and has victory. (Eternal salvation) 5:5 "Who is he that overcometh the world, but he that believeth that Jesus is the Son of God?" (Eternal salvation)

1 John 5:10 He that believeth on the Son of God hath the witness in himself: he that believeth not God hath made him a liar; because he believeth not the record that God gave of his Son.

5:10 He that believeth NOT God makes God a liar because he <u>believeth not</u> the <u>record</u> that God gave his Son. For what? To save sinners. (Eternal salvation)

1 John 5:11 And this is the record, that God hath given to us eternal life, and this life is in his Son.

5:11 The record is that God gave us <u>eternal life</u> in his Son. (Eternal salvation)

1 John 5:12 He that hath the Son hath life; and he that hath not the Son of God hath not life.

5:12 If you have the Son <u>you have life</u>. If you don't have the Son, you <u>don't have life.</u> (Eternal salvation)

1 John 5:13 These things have I written unto you that believe on the name of the Son of God; that ye may know that ye have eternal life, and that ye may believe on the name of the Son of God.

5:13 These things testify to believers that we can <u>know</u> we have eternal life. (Eternal salvation)

> *1 John 5:20 And we know that the Son of God is come, and hath given us an understanding, that we may know him that is true, and we are in him that is true, even in his Son Jesus Christ. This is the true God, and eternal life.*

5:20 Jesus the Son of God has come to give us understanding that we may <u>know</u> him. "This is the true God, and <u>eternal life</u>." (Eternal salvation)

CONCLUSION

One could cite hundreds more examples of born-again believers in this age of Grace having eternal security. One should be sufficient. If you think you could become lost, then you are calling God a liar and the Bible says there will be no liars in heaven. Could it be that some think if they know too much Bible or preaching, they will be held to a higher standard at the Judgment Seat of Christ? The Bible teaches us the standard we set for ourselves is NOT the standard we will be judged by. That standard is God's standard which will be based on His Holy Word. We had better study it and live by it to the very best of our ability.

ETERNAL SALVATION

Only because of God's abundant mercy has he allowed us underserving sinners to become children of God by the resurrection of Jesus Christ from the dead. We are heirs of God and joint heirs of Jesus Christ. We have an inheritance incorruptible, undefiled that fadeth not away, reserved in heaven for all that believe. Sealed and secure by the power of God.

2 Corinthians 5:10 For we must all appear before the judgment seat of Christ; that every one may receive the things done in his body, according to that he hath done, whether it be good or bad.

2 Timothy 2:15 Study to shew thyself approved unto God, a workman that needeth not to be ashamed, rightly dividing the word of truth.

1 Peter 1:3-5 Blessed be the God and Father of our Lord Jesus Christ, which according to his abundant mercy hath begotten us again unto a lively hope by the resurrection of Jesus Christ from the dead, To an inheritance

incorruptible, and undefiled, and that fadeth not away, reserved in heaven for you, Who are kept by the power of God through faith unto salvation ready to be revealed in the last time.

John 5:39 Search the scriptures; for in them ye think ye have eternal life: and they are they which testify of me.

THAT'S ETERNAL SALVATION!

ETERNAL SECURITY

Verily, verily, I say unto you, He that heareth my word, and believeth on him that sent me, hath everlasting life, and shall not come into condemnation, but is passed from death to life. John 5:24

SCRIPTURE REFERENCES

(Page numbers where the reference may be found are in brackets.)

GENESIS: 1:28 (24) 2:7 (24); 2:17 (25) 2:18 (25); 2:21-25 (25); 3:4-6 (26)

DEUTERONOMY: 6:4 (24)

SECOND SAMUEL: 11:3-5 (52); 11:15 (52); 11:26, 27 (52); 12:9-14 (53); 15:13, 14 (54)

PSALMS: 33:4 (20); 51:1-3 (54); 51:12 (54); 91:2 (75) 91:4, 5 (75); 119:89 (19)

PROVERBS: 30:5 (12)

ECCLESIASTES: 3:14 (20)

ISAIAH: 52:14 (40); 53:3-12 (40); 53:6 (78); 53:10 (78); 59:12, 20 (78)

EZEKIAL: 18:20a (24)

MATTHEW: 5:18 (13); 23:37 (35); 25:41, 46 (16)

MARK: 13:31 (13)

LUKE: 10:25, 27 (72); 13:34 (36), (75); 16:23a (30); 23:43 (34)

JOHN: 1:8 (29); 1:12 (38, 66); 3:3 (43); 3:15 (61); 3:18 (39, 46); 3:23 (39); 3:33 (22); 3:36 (61); 4:23,

ETERNAL SALVATION

24 (58); 4:24 (26); 5:24 (22); 5:28, 29 (33); 5:39 (84); 6:37, 39, 40 (69); 8:44, 45 (56); 10:26-29 (69); 14:6, (39); 14:15-17, 26 (57); 16:7, 8 (57); 19:3,6 (39); 19:17, 18 (40); 19:35 (22)

ACTS: 4:12 (38, 66)

ROMANS: 3:3, 4 (22); 3:4 (74); 3:10 (71); 3:23 (39,72); 3:28 (72); 5:8, 9 (65); 5:12 (29, 65); 5:21 (64); 6:16, 18 (63); 6:23 (29, 65); 8:5-11 (58); 8:35, 38, 39 (67); 8:38, 39 (63); 8:11 (44); 10:17 (9)

1st CORINTHIANS:
2:9 (32); 6:19 (57); 10:11 (21); 11:30 (56); 15:1-4 (44, 76)

2nd CORINTHIANS:
1:22 (68); 4:4 (27); 5:1 (32); 5:8 (34); 5:10 (83); 5:17 (47, 67)

GALATIANS:
3:10, 11, 13 (79)

EPHESIANS: 1:7, 13 (43); 1:7, 13, 14 (68);

PHILIPPIANS: 1-23 (32); 3:20, 21 (32); 4:7 (48)

1st THESSALONIANS:
4:17 (33)

2ND THESSALONIANS:
1:9 (15)

1ST TIMOTHY: 1:15 (39); 2:14 (26)

2ND TIMOTHY: 1:10-12 (76); 2:15 (17, 83); 3:16 (12)

SCRIPTURE REFERENCES

TITUS: 1:2 (13); 3:5 (73)

HEBREWS: 4:12 (13); 6:12 (16); 10:17 (10); 10:18 (10); 11:1 (20);11:6 (10, 20); 12:5-8, 11 (48); 12:5b-11 (50)

JAMES: 1:14-15 (28); 2:10 (28); 4:17 (28)

1st PETER: 1:3-5 (83); 1:23-25 (12); 1:18 (78); 1:18,19 (71); 5:8 (27)

2ND PETER: 1:20-21 (11); 3:9 (45)

1st JOHN: 1-8 (72); 1:9 (47, 51); 1:10 (72); 2:1, 2 (47) 2:3,4 (47); 2:15-17 (27); 2:23 (72); 3:1 (51);

INDEX

ability, 82
Absalom, 52,54
absolute, 21
accuser, 46, 47
Adam, 23, 28, 56
adultery, 51
advocate, 46
alphabet,11
An Expository Dictionary of Bible Words, 60
angels, 37, 49
annihilated, 14
apostle, 43, 75, 79
Aramaic, 18
atonement, 46
author, 17, 21,
baby, 52
Baptist Church, 15
baptized,15
bastards, 50, 55
bed, 71
begotten son, 43
behavior, 50, 70
believe. 9, 14, 59, 60, 63, 83
Believe, 5,11
believeth, 80
believing, 11, 20
Bible, 9, 11, 15, 18, 20, 27, 29, 31, 45, 59, 70, 77, 82
blood, 9, 37, 38,43, 46, 47, 61, 65, 66, 67, 70
born, 80
born again, 42
breathed, 23
buffeted, 37
burial, 75, 79
Calvary, 77
cast away, 49
cast out, 52, 68
cat, 35
chasten, 49, 50
chastened, 51, 52

chastisement, 46, 55
chicks, 74
children, 14, 83
choice, 38
Christ, 14, 45, 69, 77, 80
Christian, 9, 31, 73
church, 37
cleanses, 46
cliff, 73
comfort, 35
commandments, 28, 49, 57
commune, 23, 24
Complete Word Study Dictionary, 11
conclusion, 82
confess, 45, 46, 51
contract, 67
conscience, 56
conflict, 63
contaminated, 66
contentment, 35
continents, 18
conversations, 70
correct, 18
corruptible, 77
created, 23
cross, 31, 38, 77
crown, 37
crucified, 37
cursed, 77
damnation, 14
damned, 26
dangers, 73, 74
David, 51, 52
death, 29, 37, 55, 65, 75
deceive, 46, 70
deceived, 23
defending, 17
depression, 14
despised, 37
destruction, 14
disfigured, 38
devil, 26, 37, 46, 55, 70
dictionary, 11

SCRIPTURE REFERENCES

die, 23, 38
died, 45
disfigured, 38
dispensation, 18, 24, 56
divorced, 14
doctrines, 14
dog, 34, 35
do over, 31
earnest, 67
eat, 23
entice, 26, 27
essential, 11
eternal, 9, 11, 14
eternal damnation, 29
eternal hell, 57
eternal life, 14, 15, 29, 63,
   67, 69, 70, 81
eternal soul, 61
eternal salvation, 18, 21, 24,
   29, 35, 45, 59, 61, 63, 67,
   68, 69, 73, 76, 80, 81, 84
eternal security, 15, 20, 23, 31, 35, 36, 45, 49, 59, 65, 67, 69, 74, 79, 82, 84
eternity, 11, 14, 24, 27, 38
everlasting, 11, 14, 37, 43, 61, 68
Eve, 26
evil, 23, 71
eye, 27
faith, 20, 21, 59, 62, 70, 71
falling, 73
family, 66, 80
Father, 23, 46, 66, 73
fault, 37
fellowship, 51
filthy rags, 37
fire, 29, 73
fiery hell, 63

flesh, 27, 36
forbidden, 23
forever, 14, 18
forgive, 49
forgiveness, 43, 46, 68
food, 60
Frederick M. Lehman, 62
free ticket, 9
garden, 23
Georgia, 60
gift, 15, 18, 36, 62, 63,
glory, 15, 70, 73
God, 9, 14, 15, 17, 18, 21, 23, 27, 29, 36, 38, 43, 57, 61, 62, 65, 67, 68, 70, 73, 80, 81, 82, 83
God's ownership, 83
God the Son, 28
God's word, 59
good, 23
good works, 77
gospel, 75
grace, 24, 43, 56, 61, 62 63, 71, 82
Greek, 18
guard, 66
guide, 56
habitual sin, 46
hand, 69
happiness, 31
hardships, 75
heart, 45, 51
heaven, 9, 19, 27, 31, 37, 45, 49, 62, 71, 82
heavenly father, 46
Hebrew, 18
heir, 66, 83
hell, 14, 19, 24, 29, 37, 38, 42, 45, 62,
help meet, 23, 25
hen, 35, 74
Holy Ghost, 11, 23
holy men, 17

SCRIPTURE REFERENCES

Holy Spirit, 56, 66, 67, 75
holy word, 82
homecoming, 31
illustration, 55, 60
imagine, 31
immortality, 18, 75
imperative, 14
impossible, 20
incorruptible, 31, 77
indestructible, 21
inheritance, 83
iniquity, 77
innocent, 37
inspiration, 17
interceding 38
Isaiah, 77
Jehovah Witness, 14
Jesus, 11, 28, 35, 37, 38, 42, 45, 47, 56, 60, 61, 68, 69, 70, 71, 77, 79, 80, 81
Jesus Christ, 9, 18, 19, 31, 35, 36, 37, 43, 46, 62, 66, 67, 70, 75, 83
jot, 11
joy, 31
Judgment Seat of Christ, 82
kept by God, 76
killers, 35
King James Bible, 9, 15, 17, 18
Kingdom, 52
know, 81
know it, 79
knowledge, 9, 23, 45
lake of fire, 26, 29, 65
lawyer, 46, 70
liars, 27, 60, 61, 68, 69, 70, 81, 82
lie, 11, 59, 65, 68, 69, 70
lies, 14, 26

life, 81
limbo, 31
lion, 27
Lord, 19, 31, 36, 56, 70, 71, 72, 75, 77, 80
lose, 11
lost, 55, 57, 74
love, 35, 61, 62, 66, 74
lust, 27
master, 42
maturity, 49
mercy, 46, 83
merit, 63
Miracle of Bible Inspirations, 17
mocked, 37
modern translations, 17
murder, 51
nailing, 37
neighbor, 70
neighborhood, 34
new creature, 66
new earth, 31
new life, 46
Nicodemus, 42
nostrils, 23,
obscure, 15
obtain, 20
offering, 77
original languages, 17
pain, 38
painful, 75
paradise, 19, 31
Paul, 15, 75
payment, 38
peanut, 71
perfect, 17
perish, 43, 69
persuaded, 76
pharisee, 42
pledge, 67
pluck, 69
power of God, 83
preacher, 75
preserved, 17
pride, 27

SCRIPTURE REFERENCES

proof, 59
prophesies, 18
propitiation, 46
protection, 35, 74
punishment, 14
rebellion, 27
receive, 63
receiving, 43
record, 17
redeem, 36, 37, 77
redemption, 43
rejected, 37
religion, 42
religious, 42
remission, 37
reneged, 65
repent, 45, 51
repentant heart, 49
responsibility, 27
resurrection, 75, 83
right, 14
right hand, 38
rose again, 43
ruler, 42
safe, 74

safety, 35
salvation, 9, 11, 15, 19, 36, 70
Satan, 23, 26, 47
save, 81
saved, 29, 38, 56, 69, 70, 79
savior, 36, 56
Savior, 31, 36, 75, 80
scourged, 37
scripture, 15
sealed, 66, 67, 68, 83
second death, 65
second question, 31
secure 83
secured, 20, 23, 74, 77
security, 66, 68
security in what, 31
separated, 29
separation, 42

settled in heaven, 64
sheep, 69, 77
sin, 27, 29, 36, 38, 49, 62, 70, 71, 77
sins, 43, 46
sinner, 28
sinned, 23, 70
sinners, 15, 19, 37, 61, 70, 77, 83
sixty-six, 18
sleep, 55
Son, 23, 81
son, 52
Son of God, 80
soul, 23, 70
soul sleep, 31
sovereignty, 36, 37
spat, 37
spirit, 23, 57
Spirit, 67
Spiros Zodhiates, 11
standard, 82
street, 49, 55
Strong's Concordance, 15
study, 15, 82
suffering, 75
Sunday, 15
supper, 60, 61
teacher, 42, 75
ten commandments, 37
testimony, 38
The Defined King James Bible, 18
"The Miracle of Bible Inspiration", 17
The Old Paths Publications, 17
The Love of God, 62
thief, 31
third question, 36
three days, 38
three nights, 38
three persons, 23

SCRIPTURE REFERENCES

three questions, 20, 23
ticket, 71
time, 11
Timothy, 15
tithe, 37
tittle, 11
tomb, 38
torment, 29
tormented, 27
torture, 38
toss, 69
translation, 17
tree, 23
trials, 46
tribulations, 46
triune God, 23, 36, 66
true, 38
trust, 9, 31, 59, 63, 67, 74
trusted, 45, 55

truth, 14, 20, 23, 46
unrecognizable, 38
vine, 60
victory, 80
voice, 69
vulnerable, 74
wages, 64, 65
Waite, 18
warmth, 35
whatsoever, 80
whosoever, 80
wickedness, 27
Williams, 17
wings, 34, 35
without error, 18
word, 19
Word of God, 64
works, 63, 70
worship, 23, 31, 57
written, 21
wrong, 14

ETERNAL SALVATION

ABOUT THE AUTHOR

LEO & ELSIE LAVINKA

LEO ROBERT LAVINKA WAS BORN IN 1934. HE WAS RAISED IN MONTICELLO, FLORIDA, BUT NOT IN A CHRISTIAN HOME. AFTER HIGH SCHOOL AND ONE TOUR IN THE AIR FORCE, HE ATTENDED FLORIDA STATE UNIVERSITY BEFORE TRANSFERRING TO THE UNIVERSITY OF FLORIDA WHERE HE GRADUATED WITH A BACHELOR OF CIVIL ENGINEERING DEGREE. HE WORKED FOR

THE U.S. ARMY CORPS OF ENGINEERS IN THE JACKSONVILLE, FLORIDA, DISTRICT BEFORE TRANSFERRING TO THE DIVISION OFFICE IN ATLANTA, GEORGIA IN 1969. HE BEGAN HIS CAREER IN CONSTRUCTION AND HAD OPPORTUNITY TO PARTICIPATE IN MANY DIFFERENT MILITARY AND CIVIL ENGINEERING PROJECTS IN THE SOUTHEAST UNITED STATES, PUERTO RICO, U.S. VIRGIN ISLANDS, PANAMA CANAL ZONE, AND SOMETIMES IN OTHER CENTRAL AND SOUTH AMERICA COUNTRIES.

IN 1973 HE TRANSFERRED FROM CONSTRUCTION TO EMERGENCY MANAGEMENT WHERE HE WAS RESPONSIBLE FOR PLANNING, COORDINATING, TRAINING, AND EXECUTION OF THE CORPS' MISSIONS TO SUPPORT THE MILITARY, AND NATURAL DISASTERS RECOVERY EFFORTS. HIS RESPONSIBILITY EXPANDED TO THE MIDDLE EAST BEFORE AND DURING DESERT SHIELD, DESERT STORM, AND KUWAIT RECOVERY. HE IS THE RECIPIENT OF SEVERAL AWARDS FOR HIS SERVICE AND RETIRED IN 1999 AFTER 39 YEARS OF SERVICE TO THE U.S. GOVERNMENT.

HE WAS SAVED IN 1969 WHILE ATTENDING FORREST HILLS BAPTIST CHURCH IN DECATUR, GEORGIA, UNDER THE MINISTRY OF DR. CURTIS HUTSON AND THE WITNESSING OF A COWORKER. HE WAS ORDAINED AS A DEACON BY PASTOR HUTSON IN 1970. HE ALSO SERVED AS A DEACON AT CORINTH BAPTIST CHURCH, LOGANVILLE,

ABOUT THE AUTHOR

GEORGIA UNDER PASTOR DON RICHARDS; RETURN BAPTIST CHURCH, CLARKSVILLE, GEORGIA UNDER PASTOR WALTER BURRELL; AND IS CURRENTLY A DEACON, TREASURER, AND SECRETARY AT ZION HILL BAPTIST CHURCH, CLEVELAND, GEORGIA UNDER PASTOR NATHAN NIX, (ALL INDEPENDENT, FUNDAMENTAL BAPTIST CHURCHES).

HE HAS TAUGHT SUNDAY SCHOOL FROM ELEMENTARY TO ADULTS IN SEVERAL CHURCHES AND SERVED IN THE BUS MINISTRY AT FORREST HILLS BAPTIST CHURCH. HE HAS ALSO BEEN A JANITOR, YARD KEEPER, AND A TEACHER AT A SATELLITE CHURCH. HE HAS BEEN ACTIVE IN VISITATION PROGRAMS FROM 1970 TO THE PRESENT.

BROTHER LAVINKA IS AUTHOR OF "ANSWERED PRAYERS" AND "ARE YOU READY," WHICH ARE AVAILABLE AT:
http://www.theoldpathspublications.com/Pages/BookStore.htm

www.ingramcontent.com/pod-product-compliance
Lightning Source LLC
Chambersburg PA
CBHW061456040426
42450CB00008B/1379